PAB-0912-0154

ISBN: 978-1-4867-1396-7

Fact Checker:
Jay Johnson

Written by
Sean Kennelly

TABLE OF CONTENTS

D.Y.K.A.

DO YOU KNOW ABOUT...

How much do you know about the fifty states? Find awesome facts throughout the book as you learn more about our great nation. Just look for the D.Y.K.A. symbol!

THESE UNITED STATES

From the very beginning, America has been a land filled with adventure, unique peoples, and amazing sights.

The Early Settlements

English, French, and Spanish **settlements** dotted the shores of North America. The English claimed much of the Atlantic seacoast. The French claimed parts of the **Deep South** around what we know today as Louisiana. They also claimed land upriver through Missouri and further north in Canada. The Spanish claimed Florida and land to the southwest.

The First Thirteen and Beyond

America grew from the thirteen English **colonies**. After winning its freedom from England, the young country grew and grew. It bought land from France called the **Louisiana Purchase**. It even bought a large chunk of snowy land from Russia which we called Alaska. It also fought a war with Mexico over Texas and the western half of North America from 1846-48. In 1898, the US fought Spain to win Puerto Rico, the Philippines, and the island of Guam. After World War II, America gave the Philippines its **independence**, and now it is its own country. However, Guam and Puerto Rico are still part of the United States. They're called **US territories**.

How are States Made?

States are areas of land located within the boundary of a country such as the United States of America. Most states start out as territories of the US (except the original thirteen colonies). When enough people want to become a state, they ask to be made one. The government of the United States, or federal government, tells them to write a constitution—a set of rules or laws for their state. Once they do this, they send it back to the federal government. The government then votes to admit the state into the Union. If it is admitted, it becomes an official state of the United States. Finally, the president proclaims it a state and a new star is added to the US flag!

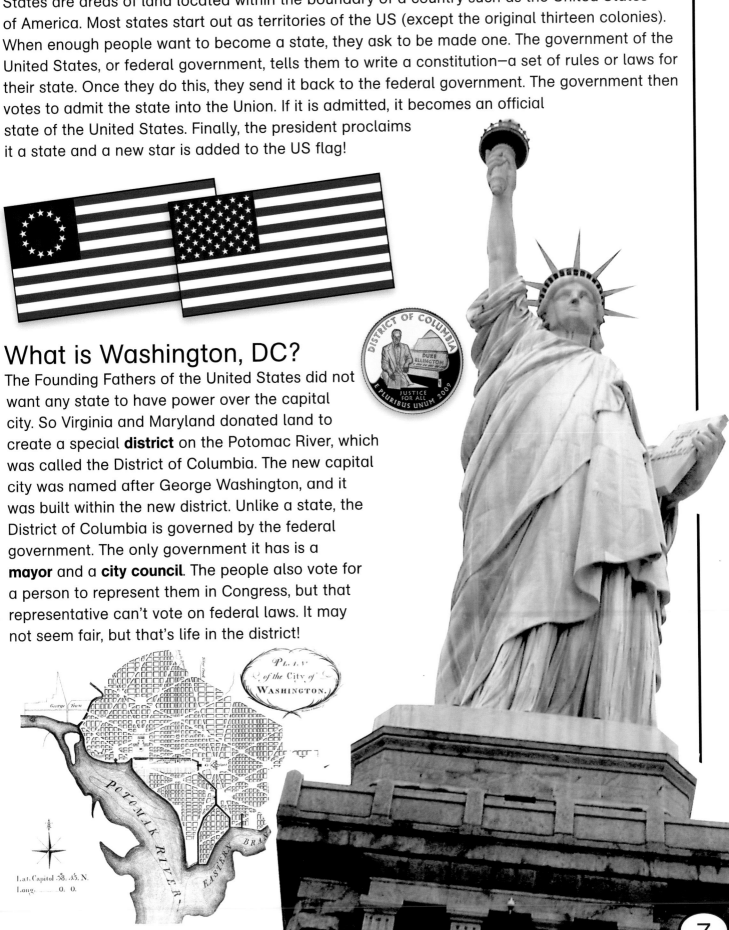

What is Washington, DC?

The Founding Fathers of the United States did not want any state to have power over the capital city. So Virginia and Maryland donated land to create a special **district** on the Potomac River, which was called the District of Columbia. The new capital city was named after George Washington, and it was built within the new district. Unlike a state, the District of Columbia is governed by the federal government. The only government it has is a **mayor** and a **city council**. The people also vote for a person to represent them in Congress, but that representative can't vote on federal laws. It may not seem fair, but that's life in the district!

THE NORTHEAST

New England

The Northeast was the site of some of the earliest settlements. Most of the people who came to America in those early years were English **Protestants**. They were seeking a place where they would be free to practice their religion without interference from the government. They also believed strongly in the voice of the people and often held town meetings. At those meetings, everyone could participate in discussing laws to govern their communities and every man could vote on them. It's no wonder they began to resent being ruled by a king across the sea who wouldn't listen to their concerns.

The people of **New England** were a tough breed tasked with taming a tough land. They learned how to get things done when they had few resources. They valued education. They knew how

important it was to work smarter. Unsurprisingly, they started a number of colleges and universities, beginning with Harvard in 1636. Yale, Dartmouth, and Brown are just a few of the other schools they started.

New England has also had a huge cultural influence on the country. Emily Dickenson, Edgar Allen Poe, Ralph Waldo Emerson, and Henry Wadsworth Longfellow are among the many writers and poets from the area. Of course, this could be partly due to the amount of time spent indoors in the winter. The bitter cold can be tough to weather unless you're busy skiing the slopes of the mountains of Vermont, New Hampshire, or Maine. Spring is filled with blossoms and green. Summers are a time to go to the beach to enjoy a good clam or lobster bake. And fall is a heavenly blanket of reds, yellows, and oranges as the leaves change color.

The Mid-Atlantic Region

The **Mid-Atlantic** is a true **melting pot** of **cultures**, cities, and natural **landscapes**. People from a wide variety of countries settled in the region. They blended their skills and turned the region into an industrial powerhouse. Some turned to mining. Others took those raw materials and forged steel and other products. Many of the products were shipped using rivers such as the Delaware River in Philadelphia or the Hudson River in New York City. They also shipped things from their many **seaports**, like the one in Baltimore.

Much of the Mid-Atlantic is heavily wooded or rural as you get farther away from the coast. The weather here is milder than New England, but the higher **elevations** can be just as cold in the winter. High humidity can also make the summers steamy unless you happen to be on the coast or on the Chesapeake Bay. Fresh crab and other seafood can always be found there, along with a gentle surf.

MARYLAND (1788)

Old Line State / Free State

Maryland was called the Old Line State by George Washington for the Maryland Line: the soldiers from the state who fought in the Revolutionary War. Being a coastal state, it is well-known for its seafood, sailing, and the US Naval Academy. The famous novel *Misty of Chincoteague* by Marguerite Henry was written about the wild ponies that reside on Assateague and Chincoteague Island. Each year, some of the ponies are rounded up and swim to the mainland to be auctioned to the public.

DELAWARE (1787)

First State / Diamond State

Delaware was the first state to **ratify** the US Constitution and thus earned the nickname First State. Some of the state's early settlers, the Swedes, built the first log cabins in America in Delaware. The capital of Dover also boasts a historic horse racing track and a NASCAR raceway nicknamed the Monster Mile. The raceway even has a glass section called the Monster Bridge, where you can sit over the track and watch the race! Of course, if you want to see some of the most amazing gardens in the country, Longwood Gardens is the place. The gardens started as a farm way back in 1700. In the 1800s, an arboretum (a garden for trees) was created by the Pierce brothers. Then in 1906, Pierre du Pont took the money he made from his family business (the famous DuPont Company) and created gardens like no other with dazzling fountains. You have to see them!

PENNSYLVANIA (1787)
Keystone State

Capital: Harrisburg
Abbreviation: PA
Population (2010): 12,702,379
Total Area: 46,054 sq. mi.
State Motto: Virtue, Liberty, and Independence
State Bird: Ruffed grouse
State Flower: Mountain laurel
Sights to See: Hershey; Pocono Mountains; Philadelphia – Liberty Bell, Independence Hall; Pittsburgh – Kennywood Amusement Park

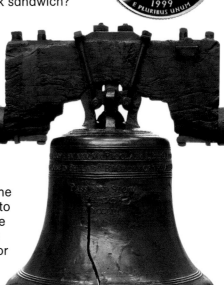

The Keystone State got its nickname from its central role in creating the new country of America. It was the place where the Declaration of Independence was signed as well as the US Constitution. In fact, Philadelphia was the first US capital. And who can resist the taste of a real Philly cheesesteak sandwich? With one of the largest populations in the United States, Pennsylvania is home to a variety of people, including the rural **Amish** and **Mennonite** communities. Pennsylvania also knows how to work hard and play hard. That explains how a city like Pittsburgh is home to industrial steel mills, winning football teams, and the roller coasters of historic Kennywood Amusement Park. But if you want to visit one of the sweetest places on Earth, you have to see Hershey, Pennsylvania. It's where one of the world's largest chocolate factories has been making sweets for over a century. Just be sure to visit Punxsutawney on February 2 for Groundhog Day!

WEST VIRGINIA (1863)
Mountain State

Originally part of Virginia, West Virginia disagreed with its brothers to the south. It was admitted to the **Union** during the Civil War. Located in the midst of the Appalachian Mountains, it is called the Mountain State because it has the highest average elevation of any state east of the Mississippi River. The land is filled with gas and coal pockets, making West Virginia one of the best coal mining sites in the world. But it's the natural beauty of West Virginia that attracts most visitors. Whitewater rafting adventures can be found on the rivers, and the high mountains offer snow skiing in the winter. Truly, West Virginia is an untamed beauty!

Capital: Charleston
Abbreviation: WV
Population (2010): 1,852,994
Total Area: 24,230 sq. mi.
State Motto: *Montani semper liberi* (Mountaineers Are Always Free)
State Bird: Northern cardinal
State Flower: Great laurel or rhododendron
Sights to See: New River Gorge; New River, Gauley River; Whitewater Rafting; Snow Skiing – Snowshoe Mountain

NEW YORK (1788)

Empire State

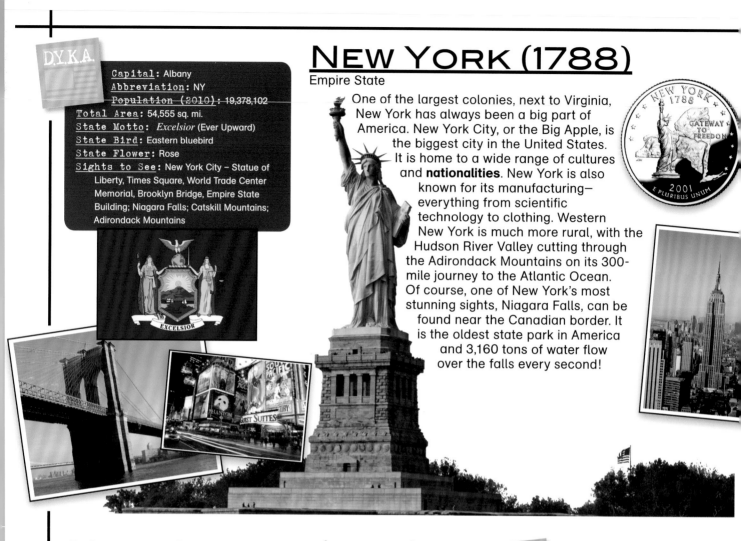

One of the largest colonies, next to Virginia, New York has always been a big part of America. New York City, or the Big Apple, is the biggest city in the United States. It is home to a wide range of cultures and **nationalities**. New York is also known for its manufacturing—everything from scientific technology to clothing. Western New York is much more rural, with the Hudson River Valley cutting through the Adirondack Mountains on its 300-mile journey to the Atlantic Ocean. Of course, one of New York's most stunning sights, Niagara Falls, can be found near the Canadian border. It is the oldest state park in America and 3,160 tons of water flow over the falls every second!

NEW JERSEY (1787)

Garden State

New Jersey was originally named after England's Isle of Jersey, but it's no island. It is surrounded by the Hudson River, the Delaware River, and the Atlantic Ocean. However, it also shares a fifty-mile land border with New York. New Jersey also has a number of fun places to visit. There are great beaches, from historic Cape May to the famous Atlantic City Boardwalk. Or you can just float down the Delaware River. New Jersey is also the site of the very first baseball game in 1846, as well as the first college football game in 1869. The first dinosaur skeleton in North America was also discovered in New Jersey. So you could call New Jersey a land of firsts!

RHODE ISLAND (1790)

Little Rhodie / Ocean State

Rhode Island was actually discovered by Italian explorer Giovanni da Verrazano in 1524. He was trying to get to France and reached Rhode Island's Narragansett Bay instead. Beautiful Narragansett Bay is home to many islands where Americans love to vacation year after year. Of course, fishing also has a long tradition in Rhode Island. Though it's true that Rhode Island is the smallest state, its capital city, Providence, is the second-biggest city in New England behind Boston, Massachusetts. The state is also home to many factories that make toys, machines, silverware, and even costume jewelry. Believe it or not, the state bird is actually a breed of chicken. But Rhode Islanders are no chickens—it's a very brave state. Back in 1776, it was the first to declare its independence from England!

D.Y.K.A.

Capital: Providence
Abbreviation: RI
Population (2010): 1,052,567
Total Area: 1,545 sq. mi.
State Motto: Hope
State Bird: Rhode Island red
State Flower: Violet
Sights to See: Narragansett – Narragansett Town Beach; Newport – Castle Hill Lighthouse; Block Island; Providence – Roger Williams National Memorial; North Kingstown – Casey Farm; Jamestown – Beavertail State Park

CONNECTICUT (1788)

Constitution State / Nutmeg State

Wherever you turn, Connecticut is filled with great places and great stories! The Old Newgate Prison in Granby was a copper mine that was turned into a prison back in the 1700s. It's said that the spooky ghosts of old prisoners and doomed miners wander its tunnels. Then there is the Mystic Seaport with its re-creation of a historic New England seaport and the Mark Twain House (the author's favorite place to live) in Hartford. You can even go inside the USS *Nautilus* at the Navy Submarine Museum in Groton. Of course, no visit to Connecticut would be complete without a visit to Yale University (founded in 1701) and its Great Hall of Dinosaurs at the Peabody Natural History Museum.

D.Y.K.A.

Capital: Hartford
Abbreviation: CT
Population (2010): 3,574,097
Total Area: 5,5543 sq. mi.
State Motto: *Qui transtulit sustinet* (He Who Transplanted, Sustains)
State Bird: American robin
State Flower: Mountain laurel
Sights to See: Mystic – Mystic Pizza, Mystic Seaport; Hartford – Harriet Beecher Stowe House, Mark Twain House; Yale University – Peabody Natural History Museum; New London – US Coast Guard Academy; East Granby – The Old Newgate Prison; Groton – US Navy Submarine Museum

MAINE (1820)

Pine Tree State

Did you know that Maine was once part of Massachusetts? It became a state in 1820 as part of the **Missouri Compromise**, which made Maine a free state to balance out the new slave state of Missouri. It was called the Pine Tree State because ninety percent of Maine is covered in forests. So if you like the great outdoors, then you might consider Maine an outdoor paradise! You could visit Acadia National Park, the nation's smallest national park; see the forty-acre Desert of Maine, an ancient glacial silt deposit; or take a ride on the Maine Narrow Gauge Railroad along Portland's waterfront, where you can see the Portland Head Light, built in 1791 (it is the oldest US lighthouse in use). And be sure to try the lobster. More lobster is caught off Maine's coast than that of any other state!

NEW HAMPSHIRE (1788)

Granite State

General John Stark of New Hampshire said, "Live free or die," on the anniversary of the Revolutionary War's Battle of Bennington. So his home state adopted the phrase as its motto. History comes alive in New Hampshire at places like The Brick Store—America's oldest general store. Or drive through the many covered bridges along the way. If you have a sweet tooth, you may want to check out Sweet Maples Sugarhouse to see how maple tree sap becomes syrup. You can also go moose watching on State Route 3, or Moose Alley as it's called. But for the best view, ride the Cog Railway to the top of Mount Washington—the highest point in the Northeast and one of the windiest on Earth! It once had a recorded wind speed of 231 mph!

VERMONT (1791)
Green Mountain State

Capital: Montpelier
Abbreviation: VT
Population (2010): 625,741
Total Area: 9,616 sq. mi.
State Motto: Freedom and Unity
State Bird: Hermit thrush
State Flower: Red clover
Sights to See: Killington; Waterbury
– Ben & Jerry's Factory; Graniteville –
world's largest active rock quarry;
Pittsford – New England Maple Museum

Ethan Allen and the Green Mountain Boys (the volunteer soldiers of Vermont) fought bravely in the Revolutionary War. They got their name from the green mountains found in the state. However, Vermont was not one of the original colonies and became the fourteenth state in 1791. Today, Vermont is known for much more. It is the biggest producer of maple syrup in the country. It also has over 100 covered bridges throughout the state. You can find the world's biggest active granite quarry in Graniteville. In the summer, you'll want to drop by the Ben & Jerry's factory in Waterbury. And if it's winter, you might want to strap on some skis and head for Killington. It's one of the top snow skiing destinations in America!

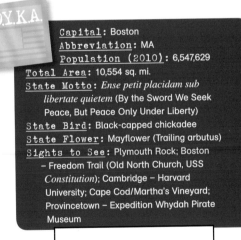

MASSACHUSETTS (1788)
Bay State / Old **Colony** State

From the day the **pilgrims** arrived at Plymouth Rock, Massachusetts has been an important part of American history. The Boston Massacre and the Boston Tea Party happened here. It's the land of Paul Revere's midnight ride where he warned that the British were coming! If you're coming by sea, you may want to visit the island of Martha's Vineyard. Many of the rich and famous (including many US presidents) vacation there every year. If you're coming by land, you may want to stop by Provincetown, where the wreck of the pirate treasure ship *Whydah* is on display with all its loot!

Capital: Boston
Abbreviation: MA
Population (2010): 6,547,629
Total Area: 10,554 sq. mi.
State Motto: *Ense petit placidam sub libertate quietem* (By the Sword We Seek Peace, But Peace Only Under Liberty)
State Bird: Black-capped chickadee
State Flower: Mayflower (Trailing arbutus)
Sights to See: Plymouth Rock; Boston – Freedom Trail (Old North Church, USS *Constitution*); Cambridge – Harvard University; Cape Cod/Martha's Vineyard; Provincetown – Expedition Whydah Pirate Museum

THE SOUTHEAST

The South

The Mason-Dixon Line is a line that was mapped out by Charles Mason and Jeremiah Dixon in 1767. The line created the borders of Pennsylvania, Maryland, Delaware, and Virginia. The states to the south took part of the name and called it **Dixie**. Dixie thrived on cotton, sugar, tobacco, and the **plantations** that grew them until the American Civil War. At the root of the war was the issue of slavery. And the South depended on slaves to do most of the work on the plantations.

At the end of the Civil War, the slaves were freed and plantations began to disappear. Smaller farms began to take their places. It wasn't until the 1900s that the South finally rose from the ashes of the Civil War to become **prosperous** again. The invention of air conditioning helped, too. People began to leave the cold winters of the North behind and head south. Today, the region is, once again, a powerhouse of **agriculture** and **industry**. And the natural beauty that has always graced the South can still be found in Dixie!

Tropical America

Not many people are aware that America extends beyond the tip of Florida to a chain of tropical islands called the Florida Keys. A key is another name for a small island. Key West is the southernmost island. To get there, you only need a car, since the entire chain is connected by US Route 1 over a series of bridges called the Overseas Highway. The longest bridge is called the Seven Mile Bridge because it's seven miles long!

The Commonwealth of Puerto Rico and the US Virgin Islands of the United States are American territories, and the people living there are US **citizens**. Many states start as territories, then become states. Puerto Rico has voted many times on becoming a state. Each time, the majority of the people decided they wanted to stay a commonwealth.

The US Virgin Islands were originally called the Danish West Indies before they were purchased by the United States. But the new name didn't change the islands much. They continue to thrive on tourists seeking a sunny Caribbean vacation.

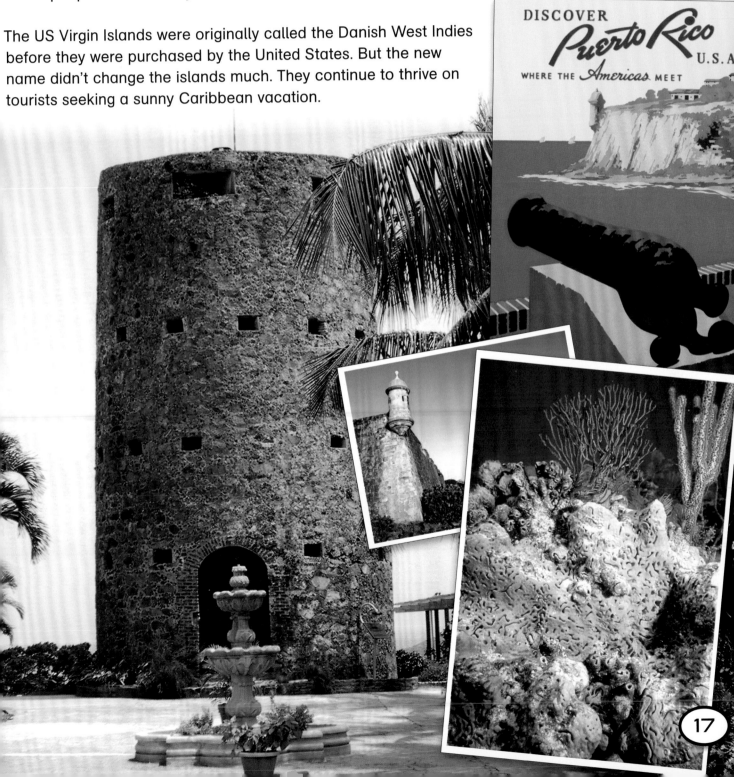

DISCOVER
Puerto Rico
U.S.A
WHERE THE *Americas* MEET

VIRGINIA (1788)
Mother of Presidents / Old Dominion

Virginia was once called the Dominion and Colony of Virginia since its **territory** made up what is now the states of West Virginia, Ohio, Kentucky, Indiana, Illinois, Wisconsin, and part of Minnesota. Many famous battles have been fought here, and Virginia has also been the home of many US presidents. George Washington, Thomas Jefferson, James Madison, James Monroe, William Henry Harrison, John Tyler, Zachary Taylor, and Woodrow Wilson all lived here. It's not surprising since Virginia is a land of beauty and variety. From Virginia Beach ("the world's longest pleasure beach") to Skyline Drive in the Blue Ridge Mountains, there are stunning sights at every turn.

NORTH CAROLINA (1789)
Tar Heel State / Old North State

Many people called North Carolina the Tar Heel State for the way its Civil War soldiers stuck to their position like they had **tar** on their heels. Yet its license plate proudly proclaims "First in Flight," since the Wright Brothers made their famous flights among the sand dunes of the **Outer Banks**. Edward Teach, the famous pirate called Blackbeard, also used the Outer Banks as his base of operations. He would often hide his ship near Ocracoke Island and attack passing boats. Today, visitors come to enjoy the beaches, the lighthouses like Cape Hatteras, or the beauty of the mountain regions. In fact, a modern recreation of a French chateau can be found near Asheville. George Vanderbilt built his famous Biltmore Mansion—the largest home in the United States, with 250 rooms!

SOUTH CAROLINA (1788)
Palmetto State

Capital: Columbia
Abbreviation: SC
Population (2010): 4,625,364
Total Area: 32,020 sq. mi.
State Motto: *Animus opibusque parati*
(Prepared in Mind and Resources) and
Dum spiro spero (While I Breathe, I Hope)
State Bird: Carolina wren
State Flower: Yellow jessamine
Sights to See: Charleston – Arthur
Ravenel, Jr. Bridge, Historic District; Fort
Sumter; Myrtle Beach; Hilton Head Island;
Chattooga River – whitewater rafting; The
Citadel; Table Rock State Park

South Carolina has always had plenty of visitors. It's said that Blackbeard once blocked the port of Charleston until it paid the ransom he demanded. During the Revolutionary War, Francis Marion spent his time in the swamps. From there he attacked British troops, who nicknamed him the "Swamp Fox." Union soldiers even made Hilton Head Island their base of operations during the Civil War. They were there to fight the Rebels who first struck at Fort Sumter. Modern visitors to South Carolina now come to the sunny shoreline of Myrtle Beach. Some come to challenge the rapids of the Chattooga River, near the Georgia border. Whatever the reason, it seems South Carolina has something for everyone!

GEORGIA (1788)
Empire State of the South / Peach State

Georgia is home to a wide range of historical and natural marvels. The old coastal port of Savannah has been called one of the most haunted cities in America. It even boasts an old pirate tavern from the 1700s! Then there's Atlanta, with its Underground—the original downtown that was built over in the 1920s. While you're there, you might want to quench your thirst at The World of Coca-Cola. However, unlike Atlanta, much of the state is rural, with farms occupying land once held by rich plantation owners in the pre-Civil War days. Stone Mountain is a sculpted rock salute to Confederate soldiers of the Civil War. And though it's called the Peach State, it is actually the world's largest producer of pecans. Kind of nutty!

Capital: Atlanta
Abbreviation: GA
Population (2010): 9,687,653
Total Area: 59,425 sq. mi.
State Motto: Wisdom, Justice, and Moderation
State Bird: Brown thrasher
State Flower: Cherokee rose
Sights to See: Savannah – City Squares, The
Pirates' House; Atlanta – The Underground, The
World of Coca-Cola, Georgia Aquarium, CNN
Center; Stone Mountain

KENTUCKY (1792)
Bluegrass State

Kentucky's Cumberland Gap was an entry point for many settlers heading into the frontier. A couple of these settlers were the parents of Abraham Lincoln, who was born in Hodgenville. If you visit the Mountain Life Museum, you can get a taste of what life was like in the early 1800s for "Honest Abe." Those settlers established farms over much of Kentucky. But below the surface is the longest known cave system in the world, called Mammoth Cave. Kentucky is also home to the famous Kentucky Derby at Churchill Downs. Baseball fans often flock to the classic Louisville Slugger factory in Louisville. Even the classic American sports car, the Corvette, is manufactured in Bowling Green!

TENNESSEE (1796)
Volunteer State

Large numbers of men from Tennessee volunteered to serve in the US Army during the War of 1812. Soon, Tennessee was known as the Volunteer State. Home to President Andrew Jackson, the state was later the site of a number of Civil War battles, such as Shiloh, Murfreesboro, and Franklin. Music soon took hold of the state, and both Memphis and Nashville are filled with singers and songwriters. Memphis, on the banks of the Mississippi River, is known as the birthplace of the blues. Elvis Presley made his home Graceland there. Nashville is world-famous as the center of country music. It's often called Music City, USA. Bristol, in the east, is also known as a music center. You could say Tennessee has a song in its heart!

ARKANSAS (1836)
The Natural State

Capital: Little Rock
Abbreviation: AR
Population (2010): 2,915,918
Total Area: 53,179 sq. mi.
State Motto: *Regnat populus*
    (The People Rule)
State Bird: Mockingbird
State Flower: Apple blossom
Sights to See: Ozark Mountains;
    Mammoth Spring; Crater of Diamonds State
    Park; Eureka Springs – Thorncrown Chapel;
    Hot Springs National Park

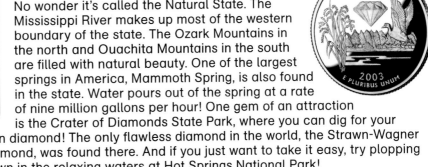

Arkansas is a land of lakes, rivers, and mountains. No wonder it's called the Natural State. The Mississippi River makes up most of the western boundary of the state. The Ozark Mountains in the north and Ouachita Mountains in the south are filled with natural beauty. One of the largest springs in America, Mammoth Spring, is also found in the state. Water pours out of the spring at a rate of nine million gallons per hour! One gem of an attraction is the Crater of Diamonds State Park, where you can dig for your own diamond! The only flawless diamond in the world, the Strawn-Wagner diamond, was found there. And if you just want to take it easy, try plopping down in the relaxing waters at Hot Springs National Park!

This Certifies That
Billy Moore
Has found a diamond in the rough from
Crater of Diamonds
Murfreesboro, Arkansas
Weight 74 pt Date 3-3-09 Color white
Tom Stolarz
Superintendent
CRATER OF DIAMONDS STATE PARK

LOUISIANA (1812)
Pelican State / Creole State / Sugar State

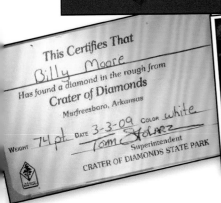

Louisiana was the first territory purchased by the young United States of America. France sold the territory, but the French influence has never left the state. The annual Mardi Gras celebration was actually brought to America by the French. Louisiana Creole, as well as Cajun French, are still spoken in the backwater **bayous** and **parishes**. They call the area Acadiana, and it even has its own flag. There's also a French Quarter of New Orleans, where a few original French colonial buildings still exist. You can even board an old-style steamboat, like the *Natchez,* and cruise up the Mississippi. Want a feel for the old plantations of the South? You may want to go to White Castle and visit the restored Nottoway Plantation. It's a real Southern belle!

Capital: Baton Rouge
Abbreviation: LA
Population (2010): 4,533,372
Total Area: 52,378 sq. mi.
State Motto: Union, Justice, and
    Confidence
State Bird: Brown pelican
State Flower: Magnolia
Sights to See: New Orleans – Bourbon
    Street, French Quarter, St. Charles Avenue,
    Jackson Square, St. Louis Cathedral; White
    Castle – Nottoway Plantation; Steamboat
    Natchez; Lafayette – Acadian Village

MISSISSIPPI (1817)

Magnolia State

Mississippi got its nickname from the state tree, the magnolia. The Mississippi River also serves as the state's western border. It is a land with fertile imaginations. The early settlers created large plantations where sugar, cotton, and tobacco were king. Many people became rich and built large homes or mansions, which can be found all across the state. During the Civil War, many battles were fought in Mississippi. The most important battle was fought in Vicksburg for control of the Mississippi River. Today, you can tour the city and even see one of the first armored ships, or ironclads, called the USS *Cairo*. Music fans may want to visit Elvis Presley's birthplace in Tupelo. Or if you want to get a taste of the Gulf Coast life, you can hop on a shrimping boat tour in Biloxi. Anywhere you go, you'll find warm Southern hospitality and charm!

ALABAMA (1819)

Heart of Dixie / Cotton State / Yellowhammer State

Alabama has been called the Heart of Dixie since the early 1800s. Cotton has always been king here. Its capital, Montgomery, was the original capital of the Confederate States of America. Jefferson Davis was actually **inaugurated** there in the state capitol building as the first (and only) president of the CSA. Since the Civil War, Alabama slowly forged a new image. They built the rockets that got men to the moon in Huntsville at the Marshall Space Center. There's even a museum where you can see real rockets, planes, and the space shuttle test vehicle, *Pathfinder*. If you like fast cars, you may want to head to Talladega where NASCAR's finest race takes place. Or just head to Mobile, where the USS *Alabama* is docked year-round.

FLORIDA (1845)
Sunshine State

Capital: Tallahassee
Abbreviation: FL
Population (2010): 18,801,310
Total Area: 58,976 sq. mi.
State Motto: In God We Trust
State Bird: Northern mockingbird
State Flower: Orange blossom
Sights to See: St. Augustine – Castillo de San Marcos; Panama City; Daytona Beach; Cape Canaveral – Kennedy Space Center; Orlando – theme parks (Walt Disney World, Universal Studios, Sea World); Tampa – Ybor City; Everglades National Park; Miami – South Beach, Bayfront Park; Florida Keys – National Maritime Sanctuary

Florida first welcomed visitors way back in 1513. Spanish explorer Juan Ponce de Leon was searching for the legendary Fountain of Youth. Spain established many settlements including St. Augustine in 1565, the oldest city in America. They call Florida the Sunshine State, but it also has some of the worst storms in the nation. Hurricanes often hit Florida shores, and it has the most lightning strikes of any state, but the visitors keep coming. They flock to Florida's beautiful beaches, theme parks, and natural wonders, such as Everglades National Park. Kennedy Space Center is also found here, along with the Daytona International Raceway. Miami and the Florida Keys enjoy tropical weather like much of the Caribbean. That means lots of rain and sun. It also means things like oranges, corn, and strawberries grow well in Florida. In fact, over half the citrus fruit grown in America is grown in the state and shipped everywhere. No matter where you live, you can always get a taste of Florida sunshine!

THE CARIBBEAN TERRITORIES
PUERTO RICO (1898)
US VIRGIN ISLANDS
ST. CROIX, ST. THOMAS, ST. JOHN (1917)

Many people are unaware that Puerto Rico is actually part of the United States. It is not a state, but rather a commonwealth with a **governor**. The island was ruled by Spain for over 400 years, but was ceded, or given, to the United States in 1898 after the Spanish-American War. The Spanish influence is still strong. Old Spanish forts are found in several places on the island. Of course, most people today love to visit Puerto Rico's beaches, bays, and rain forests.

Capital: San Juan
Abbreviation: PR
Population (2010 est.): 3,979,000
Total Area: 3,515 sq. mi.
Official Languages: Spanish; English
Form of Government: Self-governing commonwealth in association with the United States with a **Senate** and a **House of Representatives,** similar to most US states with an elected **governor**.

Capital: Charlotte Amalie
Abbreviation: VI
Population (2010 est.): 109,750
Official Language: English
Total Area: 136 sq. mi.
Form of Government: Organized unincorporated territory of the United States with one legislative house (Senate) and an elected governor.
Sights to See: Puerto Rico: San Juan – Fort San Felipe del Morro; Vieques Island – Vieques Bio Bay; El Yunque National Forest. US Virgin Islands: St. John – Trunk Bay, Virgin Islands National Park; St. Thomas – Magens Bay; Charlotte Amalie – Blackbeard's Castle; St. Croix – Buck Island Reef National Monument; Frederiksted – Fort Frederik

The US Virgin Islands were actually purchased by the United States from Denmark in 1916, during World War I. The United States wanted to keep Germany from building submarine bases there. Of course, the beauty of the islands makes it hard to think of war today. Cruise ships visit regularly. They bring lots of vacationing tourists from all over the world to sample sunny days in the Caribbean paradise!

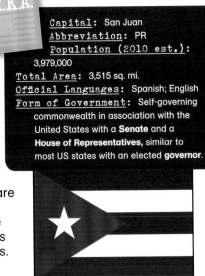

THE MIDWEST

FROM STEUBENVILLE, OHIO, TO SCOTTSBLUFF, NEBRASKA

The Heartland of America

The **Midwest** is called the Heartland for more than one reason. It's located in the middle of the country. It's also where the heart and soul of the American dream played out during the 1800s. Much of the area was a vast **plain** filled with buffalo. Settlers pushed out farther and farther West. There were clashes with Native American tribes that ended badly and both sides took losses. Sadly, the Native Americans were forced onto **reservations**, where many live to this day. Today the plains and **prairies** are filled with farms and ranches. The Heartland is the center of US agriculture. It's often called the breadbasket of America, since so much is grown here. Corn dominates, followed by wheat and other grains. Large cities are few and far between. Most of the region is dotted with small towns filled with American **ingenuity** and character. And the people tend to be open, friendly, and hardworking.

The Great Lakes

The **Great Lakes** have always been a huge industrial center for the United States. Cities like Chicago, Milwaukee, Detroit, and Cleveland sprung up along the shores of the lakes. **Waterways** and **canals** were created to link the lakes with rivers and eventually, the ocean. This meant things made there could be shipped all over the country and the world. Many large companies made the Great Lakes region their home. Companies like International Harvester, Standard Oil, United States Steel, Montgomery Ward, Sears Roebuck, Ford Motor Company, and General Motors are all located there.

The lakes themselves contain about twenty-one percent of the world's fresh water supply (and about eighty-four percent of North America's supply). Many of the areas surrounding the lakes were carved by ancient glaciers. That is part of the reason much of the land is so rich with nutrients. That makes the Great Lakes area a **fertile** farmland as well!

OHIO (1803)

Buckeye State

So what's a buckeye? It's actually the state tree of Ohio. The state is covered with trees and farmland. However, it is also a state where a lot of goods are manufactured. Ohio has many **natural resources** and energy sources, such as coal, oil, natural gas, salt, clay, and more. This means Ohioans don't have to rely on other states for the materials they need to make things. They also know how to play as hard as they work. In fact, if you like roller coasters, Sandusky is home to Cedar Point Amusement Park—the roller coaster capital of the world! Ohio is also the place to go for some really cool museums. There's the Pro Football Hall of Fame in Canton, the Rock and Roll Hall of Fame in Cleveland, and the National Museum of the United States Air Force near the Wright brothers' hometown of Dayton. There are over 360 planes and missiles on display there with a large section devoted to aviation pioneers such as Wilbur and Orville Wright. You could say Ohio has the "Wright" stuff

INDIANA (1816)

Hoosier State

Some people think a hoosier is a basketball player from Indiana. Turns out it was once a term the British used to make fun of simple people who lived in rural areas, like Indiana, back in the 1700s. Today, however, the people of Indiana are proud of their **heritage** and the name hoosier. The state is a melting pot of cultures and places. The town of Santa Claus celebrates Christmas year-round. The town of Nappanee features Amish Acres where you can see how people live a simple lifestyle without electricity. Indiana is also called the Crossroads of America since so many people travel through the state. They also race at the Indianapolis Motor Speedway. It's called the Brickyard because the track was originally paved with bricks. Whatever the season, Indiana is a state on the move!

MICHIGAN (1837)
Wolverine State / Great Lake State

Michigan is surrounded and divided by four of the five Great Lakes. Lake Superior, Lake Huron, Lake Erie, and Lake Michigan all border the state. Like several of its neighbors, Michigan is known for manufacturing. Detroit is called Motor City since it has been home to many automobile factories, dating back to the days of Henry Ford. But Ford did more than build cars. He built the nation's largest indoor/outdoor museum in Dearborn. It's filled with historic buildings like Edison's lab and the Wright brothers' bicycle shop arranged in a village. Michigan is also filled with natural beauty. Mackinac Island is a sight to behold, but you must travel by foot, bicycle, or horse and buggy—no cars are allowed! And Holland hosts the annual Tulip Festival, one of the largest flower festivals in the country. So in Michigan, you could say things are coming up tulips!

ILLINOIS (1818)
Prairie State / Land of Lincoln

Illinois is definitely the Land of Lincoln. The famous president spent much of his life here (though Kentucky gets to claim his birthplace). He's buried near his home in Springfield, where you can tour his home and presidential library. The biggest city in Illinois was once the **Mormon** city of Nauvoo in 1844. Now Chicago is the big dog and sports a host of attractions. See Sue the *T-Rex* at the Field Museum, climb ninety-nine stories to the Willis Tower skydeck for a stunning view of Chicago, or check out all the food and fun at Navy Pier (built in 1916) on Lake Michigan. No matter what you choose, most people agree that Illinois is more than just a prairie state.

ILLINOIS

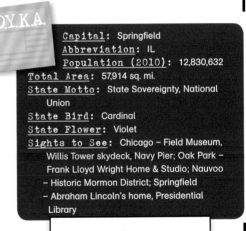

NAVY PIER

WISCONSIN (1848)

Badger State / America's Dairyland

Wisconsin celebrates its rich agricultural heritage. That's why it calls itself America's Dairyland. Wisconsin is quite famous for its dairy products, especially its cheese. It produces more cheese than any other state in America. It's also the second highest milk producer (California is the top producer). No wonder the fans of the Green Bay Packers happily call themselves "Cheese Heads." Wisconsin is also the biggest producer of water parks! You can cool off any time of the year in Wisconsin Dells. The city is home to over a dozen water parks, including one of the world's biggest—Noah's Ark. Some are indoors, some outdoors, but it's definitely a water park wonderland. So in Wisconsin, it's not all about the cheese.

MINNESOTA (1858)

North Star State / Gopher State / Land of 10,000 Lakes / Land of Sky-Blue Waters

Minnesota was the word the Dakota Indians used to describe this land of 10,000 lakes. It means land of sky-blue waters. The early settlements of Minnesota often grew around rivers where they built mills to cut lumber or to grind wheat—two big products for the state. Companies such as General Mills and Pillsbury got their start here. More than half the state lives in the Minneapolis-St. Paul area. The rest of population enjoys the more rural prairies and forests. In fact, most Minnesotans are very active. They enjoy the outdoors in places like Boundary Waters Canoe Area Wilderness. In the winter, you might find them ice fishing or hanging out at the Mall of America, a huge mall with a theme park inside! Nothing slows down the people of Minnesota!

IOWA (1846)
Hawkeye State / Corn State

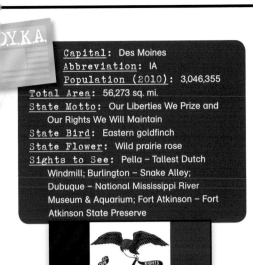

IOWA

The Hawkeye State got its nickname from Black Hawk. He was a Sauk Indian whose courage inspired many. The Sauks were some of the first to farm Iowa, but they wouldn't be the last. Many consider Iowa the food capital of the world. It produces more corn than any other state. Iowa also raises a lot of America's hogs, eggs, and soybeans. Food is not all it produces. It also harvests the power of the wind using giant wind turbines. Of course, the cities are filled with fun things to see and do. Visit Pella and you can see Dutch architecture and windmills. Burlington has one of the most crooked streets in the world called Snake Alley. Or check out what life was like on the Mississippi way-back-when in Dubuque. Stick around long enough, and Iowa just might grow on you!

MISSOURI (1821)
Show-Me State

Missouri was originally part of the Louisiana Purchase in 1803. At that time, St. Louis had already been settled by the French for almost forty years. Soon, the city was called the Gateway to the West, since explorers and pioneers often began their journeys in St. Louis. Today, the Gateway Arch stands as a very visible monument to the westward expansion of America. Missouri was also home to author Mark Twain. His boyhood home can be found in Hannibal. Twain based much of his writing on his childhood in this town. Of course, Missouri would not be much of a Show-Me State without a show-me city. Branson, in the Ozark Mountains, fits that description with a host of shows, restaurants, and attractions sure to please any visitor to Missouri.

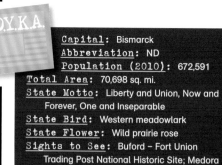
NORTH DAKOTA (1889)

Flickertail State / Sioux State / Peace Garden State

North Dakota has always been a place where different cultures encountered each other. Places like Fort Union Trading Post on the Missouri River became a place of peaceful trading between Native American tribes and the white settlers. Farms and ranches now occupy the prairies where great herds of buffalo once roamed. Buffalo can still be found in Theodore Roosevelt National Park where new herds roam the plains. In Jamestown, you can visit the National Buffalo Museum. There you can see White Cloud, the sacred white buffalo. The Lakota Indians believe the white buffalo to be a sign of peace, harmony, and balance. The International Peace Garden on the Canadian border is another place where people can come together to celebrate peace. There you can walk back and forth across the border as you enjoy the beautiful scenery and hope for the future shared by two nations!

SOUTH DAKOTA (1889)

Monument State

People have flocked to South Dakota ever since Colonel George A. Custer's men found gold in the Black Hills. Their discovery triggered a gold rush and a costly war with several Native American tribes led by Crazy Horse and Sitting Bull. The memory of his fighting spirit is carved into the rock at Crazy Horse Memorial. Not far away are the famous stone carvings of US presidents at Mount Rushmore. Historic Deadwood is the place to go if you want to get a feel for the Wild West. There are also natural monuments in South Dakota. Badlands National Park features amazing rock formations. Custer State Park is a great place to see wildlife. And no trip to South Dakota is complete without a stop at the Corn Palace in Mitchell. No wonder it's called the Monument State.

NEBRASKA (1867)
Cornhusker State / Beef State

Nebraska is one of the most rural states in the country. That's because it's always been a fertile land for farms and cattle. Nebraska actually has a greater heritage as a national highway. The Oregon and Mormon Trails both cross the state. Evidence of their visits can be seen at Scotts Bluff and Chimney Rock—both natural markers of the pioneers' journey. Even the transcontinental railroad ran through Nebraska. Omaha is still the headquarters of the Union Pacific Railroad. Of course, many decided to stay in Nebraska for the free land offered by the Homestead Act of 1862. In Beatrice, you can see an actual homestead site. The products of those homesteads continue to grow and feed America today!

KANSAS (1861)
Sunflower State / Jayhawker State

Kansas has always played a role in the growth of America. Pioneers following the Santa Fe and Oregon Trails regularly traveled through the state. Cattle ranchers from Texas drove their cattle along the famous Chisholm Trail to Abilene and Dodge City to ship them to market. Today you can stop by these cowtowns and see where the West got wild. Or visit Wichita's Old Cowtown Museum for a living history lesson with actors in costume. You can also stop by Topeka for more hands-on history with a full-size steam train at the Kansas History Museum. These days, Kansas is probably known more for agriculture. It grows much of America's wheat and beef. It is also known for wild weather. Kansas is part of an area of the United States called Tornado Alley since it has over fifty tornadoes a year. Maybe that's why the name Kansas means people of the wind!

KANSAS

THE SOUTHWEST

FROM BROKEN ARROW, OKLAHOMA, TO NOGALES, ARIZONA

Canyons, Mesas, and Tumbleweeds

The Southwest is a harsh land. It was once host to wayward outlaws and Native Americans. The Apache warrior Geronimo held off the American and Mexican armies for over a year in New Mexico. Billy the Kid and his gang rode through the territory. Even famous **gunslingers** like Wyatt Earp and Doc Holiday found the OK Corral in Tombstone, Arizona.

The land itself was hard on anyone brave enough to enter this dusty place. The early tribes of Native Americans found a way to live and thrive here. The Spanish came here in search of gold and silver. Early American settlers came here seeking a new start in a land too harsh for growing anything.

Then dams and canals were built to bring water to the deserts. Soon crops grew in the hot desert sun. Modern inventions like air conditioning and automobiles brought more and more people to the Southwest. The cities of Phoenix, Arizona, and Albuquerque, New Mexico, grew at an amazing rate. And they are still growing today.

A FREE GOVERNMENT SERV
GRAND CANYO
NATIONAL PAR
U.S. DEPARTMENT
OF THE INTERIOR NATIONAL
SERV

Cowboys, Sooners, and Indians

Texas and Oklahoma have also been tough lands to tame. Mexico had such a hard time with Comanche Indian raids that they opened the land to outsiders. Soon Americans poured into the territory. The population grew to over ten times the size it was before. Mexico tried to control the new settlers, but they were a defiant bunch. "Remember the Alamo" became their battle cry. Texas fought back and won its independence from Mexico.

Cowboys and ranchers fought to keep their cattle alive during their epic cattle drives across the state. Then oil was discovered. A new wave of people began entering Texas hoping to make a fortune. A host of oil companies sprang up such as Conoco-Phillips, Exxon-Mobil, and Marathon Oil. The oil boom fueled even more growth. Texas just keeps growing to match the big land it calls home.

Settlers in neighboring Oklahoma had their own challenges. Originally, the land was given to several Native American tribes. Soon the government decided to encourage settlement and gave the land away in great **land runs**, but keeping the land was tough. The weather was not always kind. **The Dust Bowl** of the 1930s drove many farmers and ranchers away. Those who survived are a tough but friendly breed who welcome visitors today!

ARIZONA (1912)
Grand Canyon State

Arizona is a state of contrasts. Phoenix, in the center of the state, has more days over 100°F than any other city. Flagstaff, in the north, has more days with temperatures below freezing than most cities. There are massive Native American reservations throughout the state. The biggest one, Navajo Nations, takes up an area equal in size to West Virginia. The reservation is filled with areas of unspoiled beauty, such as Monument Valley. Many famous Hollywood Westerns were filmed there and in other parts of the state. Real cowboys also lived here. Tombstone was where the famous gunfight at the OK Corral happened. Natural wonders like Meteor Crater, a huge impact crater, cover the state. Ruins of ancient cliff dwellings can be seen at Montezuma Castle National Monument. You can even walk across the famous London Bridge (moved from England) at Lake Havasu City. Arizona is definitely grand. And it even has a Grand Canyon to prove it!

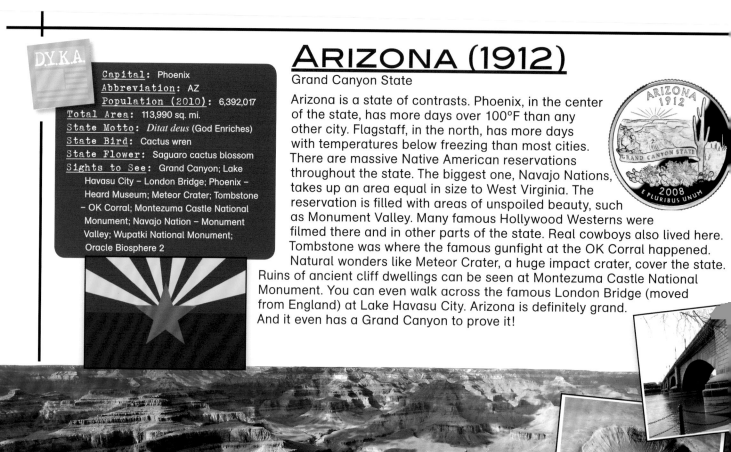

NEW MEXICO (1912)
Land of Enchantment / Sunshine State

It's rumored that New Mexico's nickname, Land of Enchantment, originally started with the Santa Fe Railroad, yet people have been enchanted by New Mexico for centuries. The Pueblo Indians made their home here in places like Chaco Canyon. The Spanish **conquistadors** lived in the Palace of Governors in Santa Fe. The famous gunslinger Billy the Kid lived here and died at Maxwell Ranch, where they have a museum about his life. Even aliens seem to be attracted to New Mexico. Tales of their visits can be seen at Roswell's UFO Museum. Carlsbad Caverns even offers enchantment a mile below the surface. It seems New Mexico is more than enchanting. For some, it's irresistible.

TEXAS (1845)

Lone Star State

Texas is one of a few states that can claim to have once been an independent country. That is why it's called the Lone Star State. The single star reminds it of its struggle for independence from Mexico. The Alamo Mission in San Antonio was one place where it battled. Eventually, it won and chose to become part of the United States. It is the second-biggest state in America—only Alaska is bigger. Amazingly, cattle ranches and farms cover much of the state. The cities are Texas-big with Houston (fourth), San Antonio (seventh), and Dallas (ninth) in the top ten of America's biggest cities. Johnson Space Center in Houston is also the control center for all manned space flights. They even have beaches, such as South Padre Island, on the Gulf Coast. But there's nothing quite like a good dance at Guene Hall. It's Texas' oldest continually-running dance hall, built in 1878. Texas has it all!

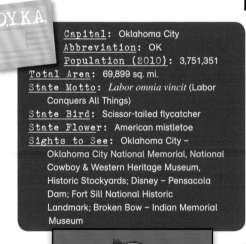

OKLAHOMA (1907)

Sooner State

What's a Sooner? Well, the government set times when a settler could race for and claim free land in Oklahoma. People who broke the rules and secretly crossed the border early were called Sooners. And the name stuck! Unfortunately, Oklahoma was also a land of tears. Many Native Americans were forced to move to Oklahoma. They called the trail they traveled the Trail of Tears. Broken Bow has a museum that tells their story. You can also see the grave of the famous Apache warrior, Geronimo, at Fort Sill. Today's Sooners live in a land filled with twisters (it's part of Tornado Alley). The legacy of the modern cowboy can be found in Oklahoma City at the National Cowboy Hall of Fame and the historic Stockyards City. Through it all, you can say one thing about Oklahoma: its future will always look OK.

OKLAHOMA

THE WEST

The Wild West

"Go West" was a cry heard by many of the early pioneers. They ventured into unknown territories hoping to find land and prosperity. What they often found was a lawless land and a fight against the elements.

Of course, the West Coast had been settled by the Spanish in the 1700s, but lands in-between were ruled by a gun. The frontier was no place for the weak. Only the strong survived. Gradually, as law and order were established, along with the railroads, the West was opened up!

Today, it is a land of splendor and industry. Silicon Valley in Northern California is a land of technological wonder, yet it's the natural wonders that capture the imagination of most visitors to the West.

New Frontiers

Alaska and its wild territory became part of America back in 1867. Its distance from the rest of the United States kept its wilderness pristine. Then the late 1800s brought a gold rush. Years later, oil was discovered. Huge pipelines were built to bring this "black gold" to a hungry market. Yet, it's the Alaskan landscapes that are the main attraction today.

Hawaii was an entirely different frontier. Originally, it was a country ruled by the grand king of the islands, Kamehameha the Great. Gradually, people came to the islands to work in the sugar cane and pineapple fields. Then Queen Liliuokalani was overthrown in 1893 and the country was eventually **annexed** by the United States. Luckily, the islands still retain their culture and beauty. From the Napali Coast to the summit of Mauna Kea, the Hawaiian Islands are a sight to behold!

Guam, the Northern Mariana Islands, and American Samoa are also Pacific Island gems. Guam and the Northern Mariana Islands were both inhabited by the native Chamorros, and the native language is still spoken today on both islands. American Samoa was originally claimed by the United States, but has been allowed to govern itself since 1967. But there is one thing all three territories share—they are all a taste of paradise!

WYOMING (1890)
Equality State

D.Y.K.A.

Capital: Cheyenne
Abbreviation: WY
Population (2010): 563,626
Total Area: 97,813 sq. mi.
State Motto: Equal Rights
State Bird: Western meadowlark
State Flower: Indian paintbrush
Sights to See: Yellowstone National
   Park; Jackson Hole; Grand Tetons National
   Park; Hole-in-the-Wall; Devils Tower National
   Monument; Cheyenne; Cody – Buffalo Bill
   Museum; Laramie – Fort Laramie

Wyoming has always been a land of wonders. Yellowstone National Park was first described by explorer John Colter as a place of "fire and brimstone" in 1807. Most folks thought he was crazy. Turns out he was telling the truth! Today, people from around the world flock to Yellowstone to see wildlife, hot springs, mud pots, and geysers. Others come to see Wyoming's mountains, such as the Grand Tetons. Some visit ancient volcanic features like Devils Tower in the northeastern corner of the state. Western outlaws, like Butch Cassidy and the Sundance Kid, came to Wyoming to hide out at Hole-in-the-Wall in the Big Horn Mountains. Even the famous showman "Buffalo Bill" Cody liked the state so much he started a town called Cody. That's just the natural attraction that is Wyoming!

COLORADO (1876)
Centennial State

Colorado is called the Centennial State since it was admitted in 1876, the 100th anniversary of the United States. Colorado is host to a variety of landscapes. To the south are deserts and Great Sand Dunes National Park. To the east are flat prairies and farmland. To the west are canyon lands, like Dinosaur National Monument, where fossils are found, or places like Mesa Verde National Park, where ancient cliff dwellings can be explored. But the heart of Colorado is its mountains. Over half the state is covered with rocky peaks. More than 800 mountains are over 10,000 feet high. And you don't have to be a mountain climber to enjoy them. Pike's Peak (elevation 14,115 feet) actually has a road to the top! And the view from the summit inspired Katharine Lee Bates to write the words to "America the Beautiful."

D.Y.K.A.

Capital: Denver
Abbreviation: CO
Population (2010): 5,029,196
Total Area: 104,094 sq. mi.
State Motto: *Nil sine numine* (Nothing
   Without Providence)
State Bird: Lark bunting
State Flower: White and lavender
   columbine
Sights to See: Denver – US Mint;
   Golden – Colorado Railroad Museum;
   Dinosaur – Dinosaur National Monument;
   Pike's Peak; Cortez – Mesa Verde National
   Park; Colorado Springs – US Air Force
   Academy; Estes Park – Rocky Mountain
   National Park; Great Sand Dunes National
   Park and Preserve; Royal Gorge

UTAH (1896)

Beehive State / Crossroads of the West

Capital: Salt Lake City
Abbreviation: UT
Population (2010): 2,763,885
Total Area: 84,897 sq. mi.
State Motto: Industry
State Bird: California seagull
State Flower: Sego lily
Sights to See: Salt Lake City – Temple Square; Park City; Promontory Point – Golden Spike; Arches National Park; Rainbow Bridge National Monument; Zion National Park; Bryce Canyon National Park; Lake Powell; Bingham Canyon Mine

The name Utah comes from the Ute Indians who lived in the state. The name means people of the mountains. Anyone who's been to Utah can tell you about the mountains and the greatest snow on Earth found at the many ski resorts. Utah was settled largely by **Mormon** pioneers led by Brigham Young in the 1800s. Through their efforts, the desert valleys were turned into productive farmland. They also built a solid granite temple, which can be seen in Salt Lake City today. The city also hosted the 2002 Winter Olympics. It was a natural fit with a state that is known for outdoor recreation. National parks like Zion, Bryce Canyon, and Arches draw thousands of visitors each year. Some even visit Promontory Point, where the transcontinental railroad was completed. No wonder they call Utah the Crossroads of the West.

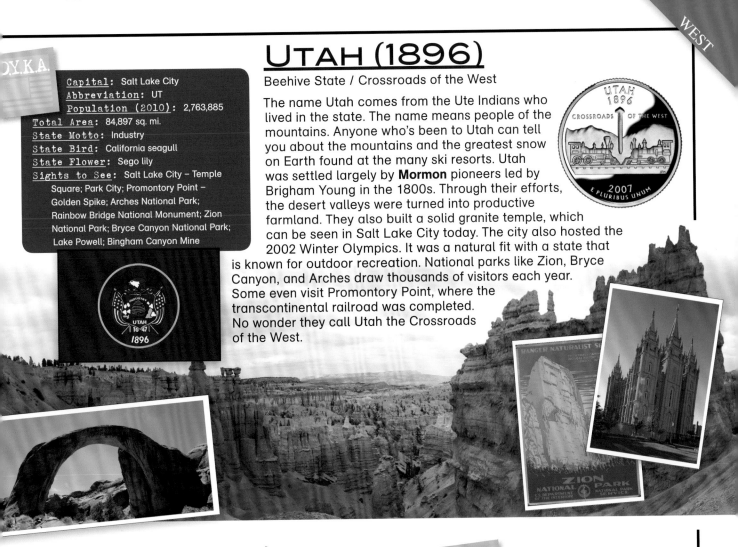

NEVADA (1864)

Silver State / Sagebrush State /
Battle Born State

The Silver State got its name long before casinos dotted the desert floor. The discovery of silver at the Comstock Lode in 1859 attracted thousands of people. Just before the discovery, Mormons had built a fort in what would become Las Vegas. Nevada was soon a state and things were never the same. Mining continued to play a large part in the state's growth, but the largest growth came when the government came to town. Boulder, or Hoover Dam, was built in 1935. It harnessed the power of the Colorado River, providing power to the Las Vegas area and beyond. It also created the biggest human-made lake in America, Lake Mead. Other government projects and military bases came to the state and brought more people with them. Soon gambling and casinos were added to the mix. Before long, Nevada became the bright and shiny tourist destination it is today!

Capital: Carson City
Abbreviation: NV
Population (2010): 2,700,551
Total Area: 110,572 sq. mi.
State Motto: All for Our Country
State Bird: Mountain bluebird
State Flower: Sagebrush
Sights to See: Las Vegas; Reno; Boulder Dam; Lake Mead; Lake Tahoe

WASHINGTON (1889)

Evergreen State / Chinook State

Washington is the only state named after a US president. It is definitely the Evergreen State. Much of the state is made up of temperate rain forests and old growth trees. Olympic National Park is one place you can see such evergreens. You can also see mountains and ancient glaciers in many places, including Mount Rainier National Park. Natural adventure can be found in places like Mount St. Helen's National Volcanic Monument. There, you can see a volcano that literally blew its top in 1980. However, the coast is where much of Washington's business happens. Logging, fishing, and high-tech software companies all call the **Puget Sound** area home. Seattle is the biggest of the cities. Over half the state's population lives, works, and plays there. They go to places like the Space Needle (605 feet) or Pioneer Square, where you can see a real totem pole. Just remember to bring an umbrella; the Washington coast is one of the rainiest places in America!

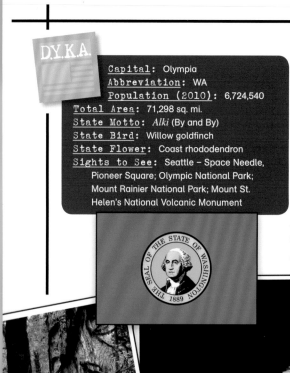

OREGON (1859)

Beaver State

Explorers Lewis and Clark navigated the Columbia River in their famous journey to map the Louisiana Purchase. They weren't the first adventurers to reach Oregon, and they weren't the last either. Astoria began as Fort Astoria. It was named after John Jacob Astor of New York, who funded the new settlement, where they traded in furs. Many of the furs came from beavers, which is where the state gets its nickname.

Today's Oregon travelers come for a variety of reasons. Some want to see nature's handiwork at Crater Lake National Park, Mount Bachelor, or Multnomah Falls in Troutdale. You can even snow ski year-round at Mount Hood due to its many glaciers. On the coast there are wonders such as the Heceta Head Light or Sea Lion Cave, both near Florence. Sea Lion Cave is one of the great sea cave grottoes of the world with a 125-foot-high vaulted stone ceiling and sea lions!

STATE OF OREGON
1859

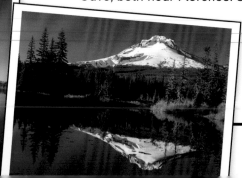

IDAHO (1890)
Gem State

Capital: Boise
Abbreviation: ID
Population (2010): 1,567,582
Total Area: 83,569 sq. mi.
State Motto: *Esto perpetua* (Let It Be Perpetual)
State Bird: Mountain bluebird
State Flower: Syringa (Lewis' mock orange)
Sights to See: Twin Falls – Shoshone Falls; Sun Valley; Craters of the Moon National Monument; Ketchum – Ketchum, Sun Valley Heritage Museum; Bruneau Dunes State Park

Every known gemstone has been found in the state of Idaho. That's how it got the name Gem State. In fact, the rare star garnets can only be found in two places on the planet—India and Idaho. Of course, they're not the only Idaho gems. Astronauts used to train on the lava landscapes at Craters of the Moon National Monument since it is very similar to the moon. Today, visitors can explore the other-worldly landscape filled with cinder cones and lava tube caves. Sun Valley in central Idaho is one of the state's snow skiing and recreation gems. Shoshone Falls in Twin Falls is another overlooked gem. At a height of 212 feet, it is actually higher than the more famous Niagara Falls. And few people know that Lewistown, Idaho, is a true seaport. The Snake and Columbia Rivers actually connect it to the Pacific Ocean. Of course, Idaho's most famous gem is the potato that it ships to destinations all over the country!

MONTANA (1889)
Big Sky Country / Treasure State

Montana has two nicknames for the two distinct sections of the state. The west gives Montana its name as a Treasure State. One of the largest US gold deposits was found at Adler Gulch (now called Virginia City). Glacier National Park with its beautiful lakes and mountains is a national treasure. Lewis and Clark Caverns is another treasure that, strangely enough, was never visited by the famous explorers. They did visit Pompey's Pillar, though. Like many pioneers and explorers, William Clark carved his name into the sandstone pillar, which can still be seen to this day. Not far away is the site of Custer's Last Stand at Little Bighorn Battlefield National Monument. Big Sky Country refers more to eastern Montana with its prairies and flat plains. Of course, you could call the whole state dinosaur country for the fossils found throughout!

Capital: Helena
Abbreviation: MT
Population (2010): 989,415
Total Area: 147,040 sq. mi.
State Motto: *Oro y plata* (Gold and Silver)
State Bird: Western meadowlark
State Flower: Bitterroot
Sights to See: Glacier National Park; Little Bighorn Battlefield National Monument; Pompey's Pillar National Monument; National Bison Range; Lewis and Clark Caverns

MONTANA

SEE AMERICA
WELCOME TO MONTANA
UNITED STATES TRAVEL BUREAU

CALIFORNIA (1850)
Golden State

D.Y.K.A.

Capital: Sacramento
Abbreviation: CA
Population (2010): 37,253,956
Total Area: 163,695 sq. mi.
State Motto: *Eureka (I Have Found It)*
State Bird: California valley quail
State Flower: California poppy
Sights to See: Yosemite National Park;
Sequoia National Park; Kings Canyon
National Park; San Francisco – Golden Gate
Bridge, Fisherman's Wharf, Alcatraz Island;
Old Spanish Missions; El Camino Real; Big
Sur; Disneyland; Hollywood – Grauman's
Chinese Theater, Walk of Fame; Santa
Monica Pier; San Diego Zoo

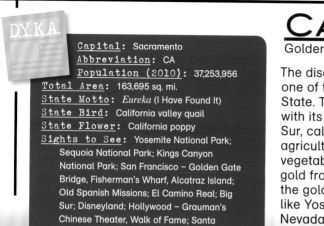

The discovery of gold at Sutter's Mill in 1848 is just one of the reasons California is called the Golden State. The golden sands of the 840-mile shoreline with its beautiful beaches, like Malibu or Big Sur, call to many. The Central Valley produces agricultural gold with its variety of fruits and vegetables. California also produces box office gold from its dream factories in Hollywood. Of course, the gold standard for outdoor beauty is found in places like Yosemite and Sequoia/Kings Canyon National Parks or the Sierra Nevada Mountains at Lake Tahoe. Tourists can't help but be drawn to classic attractions like Disneyland, the historic chain of Spanish Missions, the Santa Monica Pier, and the Golden Gate Bridge in San Francisco. California is truly gold, from its rich history to its land and sunny weather. Even if there is an occasional earthquake, the rush for California gold continues today!

CALIFORNIA REPUBLIC

ALASKA (1959)
The Last Frontier

Alaska is truly the Last Frontier in America. One look at Denali National Park and you'll know you're in a whole new world. The state is home to a host of wildlife, including caribou, moose, bears (grizzly, black, and polar), wolves, eagles (bald and golden), seals, and sea otters. Alaska is the biggest state in the Union. Many visitors arrive on cruise ships to see icebergs calve (break away) into Glacier Bay or the **fjords** of Kenai Fjords National Park. Or you could use the original native Aleut method of travel—dog sleds! Of course, you may just want to watch annual Iditarod Trail Sled Dog Race without enduring the harsh winter weather. And if you want to get a feel for the Klondike Gold Rush of 1897, you can visit El Dorado Gold Mine in Fairbanks. In order to see Alaska with a new perspective you need to stop at the Alaska Native Heritage Center in Anchorage. They may even teach you to say *"Aang-Aleut,"* which is Aleut for "Hello!"

D.Y.K.A.

Capital: Juneau
Abbreviation: AK
Population (2010): 710,231
Total Area: 665,384 sq. mi.
State Motto: North to the Future
State Bird: Willow ptarmigan
State Flower: Alpine forget-me-not
Sights to See: Denali National Park/
Mount McKinley (Denali); Iditarod Trail Sled
Dog Race; Kenai Fjords National Park;
Glacier Bay; Kodiak Island; Chugach State
Park; Fairbanks – El Dorado Gold Mine;
Anchorage – Alaska Native Heritage Center

HAWAII (1959)
Aloha State

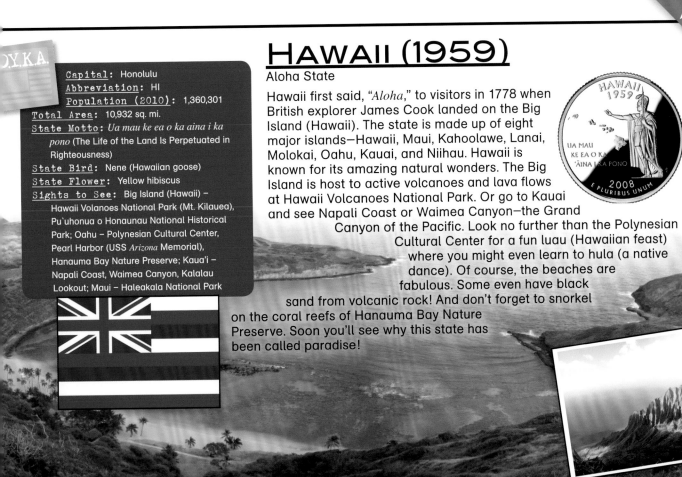

Hawaii first said, "*Aloha*," to visitors in 1778 when British explorer James Cook landed on the Big Island (Hawaii). The state is made up of eight major islands—Hawaii, Maui, Kahoolawe, Lanai, Molokai, Oahu, Kauai, and Niihau. Hawaii is known for its amazing natural wonders. The Big Island is host to active volcanoes and lava flows at Hawaii Volcanoes National Park. Or go to Kauai and see Napali Coast or Waimea Canyon—the Grand Canyon of the Pacific. Look no further than the Polynesian Cultural Center for a fun luau (Hawaiian feast) where you might even learn to hula (a native dance). Of course, the beaches are fabulous. Some even have black sand from volcanic rock! And don't forget to snorkel on the coral reefs of Hanauma Bay Nature Preserve. Soon you'll see why this state has been called paradise!

D.Y.K.A.

Capital: Honolulu
Abbreviation: HI
Population (2010): 1,360,301
Total Area: 10,932 sq. mi.
State Motto: *Ua mau ke ea o ka aina i ka pono* (The Life of the Land Is Perpetuated in Righteousness)
State Bird: Nene (Hawaiian goose)
State Flower: Yellow hibiscus
Sights to See: Big Island (Hawaii) – Hawaii Volanoes National Park (Mt. Kilauea), Pu'uhonua o Honaunau National Historical Park; Oahu – Polynesian Cultural Center, Pearl Harbor (USS *Arizona* Memorial), Hanauma Bay Nature Preserve; Kaua'i – Napali Coast, Waimea Canyon, Kalalau Lookout; Maui – Haleakala National Park

THE PACIFIC TERRITORIES
Guam (acquired 1898), Northern Mariana Islands (admitted 1978, US Commonwealth)
American Samoa (acquired 1899, self-governing since 1967)

D.Y.K.A.

GUAM
Capital: Hagåtña (formerly Agaña)
Population (2010 est.): 187,000
Official Languages: Chamorro; English
Total Area: 217 sq. mi.
Head of State: President of the United States
Form of Government: Self-governing, organized, unincorporated territory of the United States with one legislative body (Legislature) and a governor.
Monetary Unit: US Dollar

NORTHERN MARIANA ISLANDS
Seat of Government: Saipan
Population (2010 est.): 48,300
Official Languages: Chamorro; Carolinian; English
Total Area: 176.5 sq. mi.
Head of State: President of the United States
Form of Government: Self-governing commonwealth in association with the United States, having two legislative houses (Senate, House of Representatives)
Monetary Unit: US Dollar

AMERICAN SAMOA
Capital: Fagatogo (legislative and judicial) and Utulei (executive)
Population (2010 est.): 65,900
Official Languages: English; Samoan
Total Area: 77 sq. mi.
Form of Government: Unincorporated and unorganized territory of the United States with two legislative houses (Senate and House of Representatives) and a governor
Monetary Unit: US Dollar

Guam was once part of Spain, and its influence can be seen in the Dulce Nombre De Maria Cathedral Basilica. The island hosts major US military bases today. It's also part of Typhoon Alley. Many homes are made with reinforced concrete to withstand the hurricane-strength storms. And if you want a taste of the native culture, be sure to visit the Chamorro Village Market on Wednesdays for food and entertainment that can only be found in Guam!

The Northern Mariana Islands are made up of fifteen islands just north of Guam. Several of the islands have active volcanoes on them. The beaches and the coral reefs are beautiful, especially on Mañagaha Island where the famous Caroline Islands Chief Aghurubw is buried!

American Samoa shares many of the same features and culture as its cousin, the country of Samoa (also called Western Samoa). In fact, the traditional birthplace of Samoa is found within the territory at the Manu'a Islands. They are part of the National Park of American Samoa. It is the only national park south of the equator!

GLOSSARY

Agriculture – The business of farming or raising animals for food

Amish – Strict Mennonite groups, known for their simplistic lifestyle, mostly located in Pennsylvania, Ohio, Indiana, and Canada, who originally followed Jakob Ammann, a 17th century Swiss Mennonite bishop

Annex – To incorporate an area of land into a larger state, as in the United States' annexation of Texas

Bayou – A swampy or slow-moving body of water and the land surrounding it; often found in the Deep South in states like Louisiana

Canal – A human-made waterway used for navigation or irrigation

Citizen – A native or naturalized inhabitant of a place or nation

City council – An elected, lawmaking group of people who help run a city or town

Colony – An area inhabited by a group of people who have ties to another country

Commonwealth – A large area of land with borders within a country that is like a state

Conquistadors – Spanish conquerors of Mexico and other parts of North and South America

Culture – Ideas, activities, and traditions of a group of people

Deep South – The most southern states of the southeastern US, namely Alabama, Georgia, Mississippi, South Carolina, and Louisiana

District – An area similar to a state, but smaller, such as the District of Columbia

Dixie – A nickname for the southeastern states; adopted from the Mason-Dixon line that created the state boundaries between the free state of Pennsylvania and the slave state of Missouri

Elevation – How high or low a land mass is

Federal government – The national government of a country

Fertile – Something that is able to produce or make more of something (for example: fertile soil produces more crops)

Fjords (pronounced "fee-yords") – Long, narrow arm of the sea with steep cliffs or mountains on either side

Governor – The leader of a state or territory

Gunslinger – A person known for their skill with a gun

Great Lakes – The name of five large lakes (Lake Superior, Lake Michigan, Lake Huron, Lake Erie, and Lake Ontario)

Heritage – Aspects of cultural history like artifacts, traditions, and languages that are passed down through generations

House of Representatives – An elected, lawmaking group based on the number of people living in each state, which allows states with more people to have more votes on new laws

Inaugurated – Officially introduced to a new job or position, such as president of the United States

Independence – The state of being no longer associated with or controlled by another entity

Industry – Making or manufacturing things like cars, computers, steel, or glass, often in a factory

Ingenuity – The ability to come up with clever or creative ways of doing or making things

Land run – An event in the 1800s in which certain land in the US became available for purchase, resulting in a rush of people trying to acquire the land first

Landscape – An area of land, including all plants and natural features

Louisiana Purchase – Land bought from France in 1803 that doubled the size of the United States; Louisiana and all, or part, of over fourteen other states were created from the land

Mayor – The elected leader of a city

Melting pot – A term used to describe many people representing different countries, races, and religious beliefs working together to form a shared community or country

Mennonite – A member of a Protestant faith, known for their simplistic lifestyle, named after Menno Simons, a 16th century Frisian religious leader

Mid-Atlantic – An area around the central Atlantic coast including Virginia, West Virginia, Delaware, Maryland, New Jersey, Pennsylvania, and New York

Midwest – An area of the north central US that is made up of a dozen states from Ohio in the East to the Dakotas in the West

Missouri Compromise – A law passed in 1820 that allowed Missouri to be admitted as a slave state and Maine to be admitted as a free state with no slavery allowed further north in the territories, such as Nebraska or Kansas

Mormon – The nickname for a member of the Church of Jesus Christ of Latter-day Saints

Nationality – Membership to a particular country or nation

Natural resources –Materials, such as land, forests, water, or minerals (like gold or iron), found in nature

New England – The northeast area of the United States, which includes the states of Vermont, Connecticut, New Hampshire, Rhode Island, Massachusetts, and Maine

Outer Banks – A 200-mile string of barrier islands off the coast of North Carolina where the Wright Brothers made their first powered flight

Parish – Another name for a county, typically found in the state of Louisiana

Pilgrims – Protestant settlers that came across the Atlantic Ocean seeking religious freedom in a new land

Plain – An area of land that is mostly flat, for example the areas east of the Rocky Mountains in the central US are called the Great Plains

Plantation – A very large farm with lots of workers, often in the southern states; most workers were slaves until they were freed during the Civil War

Prairie – A grassy, mostly flat area of land that has few trees, much like the central United States

Prosperous – Successful

Protestant – A member of any Christian faith that protested the changes in the original Catholic, Anglican, or Eastern Orthodox Churches

Puget Sound – A sound (or a long passage of water connecting two large bodies of water) located in the Pacific Ocean in northwest Washington State

Ratify – To formally approve or affirm something

Reservation – A piece of land governed by and inhabited by American Indians (although not all American Indians live there)

Seaport – A town or city on an ocean or river connected to the ocean where goods are loaded or unloaded on ships to be transported to other places

Senate – An elected, lawmaking group made up of two representatives from each state, giving all states an equal vote on new laws

Settlement – A place or region that is newly settled or established

Tar – A thick, black, sticky substance made of tree sap that drips out of wood when it is heated to a high temperature and turned into wood coal

The Dust Bowl – A period of very bad dust storms in North American prairies during the Great Depression

US territory – An area, like a state, that is also part of the United States

Union – Another name for all the states that have joined together to form the United States of America

Waterway – A river or canal, sometimes with small movable dams (called locks) that allow large ships to travel from areas like the Great Lakes to the ocean

INDEX